THE WORSHIP HYMNS FOR ORGAN

Wedding Collection

arranged by **Carolyn Hamlin**

table of contents

For A. George Kohl

Love Divine, All Loves Excelling

Sw. Oboe 8', Rohr Bourdon 8', Trem.
Gt. Harmonic Flute 8', Spitzflute 4'
Ch. Erzahler 8', Erzahler Celeste 8', Gedeckt 8'
Ped. Lieblich Gedeckt 16', Gedeckt 8'

BLAENWERN
William Penfro Rowlands
Arr. by Carolyn Hamlin (ASCAP)

13
Ch.
17
Gt.
21
Ch.
Sw.
25
Ch.

Sw. Viola 8', Viola Celeste 8', Flute Celeste II 8'
Gt. Gamba 8', Gemshorn 8', Flute 8', Sw. to Gt.
Ch. Gedeckt 8', Krummhorn 8', Trem.
Ped. Violone 16', Lieblich Gedeckt 16', Sw. to Ped. 8'

Sw. Bourdon 8', Flute 4'
Gt. Prin. 8', Harm. Fl. 8', Fl. 4', Sw. to Gt. 8', Ch. to Gt. 8'
Ch. Gedeckt 8', Koppelflute 4'
Ped. Bourdon 16', Flute 8', Ch. to Ped. 8'

Sw. Gedeckt 8', Flute 4', Principal 4', Piccolo 2'
Gt. Diap. 8', Harm. Fl. 8', Octave 4', Fifteenth 2', Mix. IV, Sw. to Gt. 8', Ch. to Gt. 8'
Ch. Gedeckt 8', Flute 4', Principal 4'
Ped. Bourdon 16', Violone 16', Flute 8', Gt. to Ped. 8'

Much broader

Sw. +Mix. IV, Waldhorn 16'
Gt. +Double Trumpet 16'
Ped. +Diapason 16', Bombarde 16'
61
66
70
slight rit.
75
Opening registration
Gt.
a tempo
Sw.
slowing to end
Gt.
Ped. +Soft 32'

For the wedding of Tim and Katy Whitson

Processional on a Sicilian Hymn

(O Sanctissima)
(Oh, How Joyful)
(Savior, Like a Shepherd Lead Us)
(Lord, Dismiss Us with Thy Blessing)

Sw. Trumpet 8', Octave 4'
Gt. Diap. 8', Harm. Flute 8', Spitzflote 4', Ch. to Gt. 8'
Ch. Gedeckt 8', Principal 4', Koppelflute 4'
Ped. Bourdon 16', Violone 16', Ch. to Ped. 8'
Alternate MIDI registrations enclosed in boxes throughout

SICILIAN MARINERS
The European Magazine and London Review, 1792
Arr. by Carolyn Hamlin (ASCAP)

Sw. Trumpets
Gt. Strings, Harpsichord
Ped. Tuba

10
13
16
20
Gt.

Sw. Bourdon 8', Principal 4', Piccolo 2', Mix. IV, Waldhorn 16', Trumpet 8', Clarion 4'
Gt. Diapason 8', Harmonic Flute 8', Octave 4', Sw. to Gt. 8'
Ped. Bourdon 16', Violone 16', Octave 8', Sw. to Ped. 8'

Sw. Trumpets, Trombones
Gt. Bassoon, Strings

32
35
Gt.
39
42
poco rit.

Sw. Viola 8', Bourdon 8', Principal 4', Piccolo 2', Mix. IV, Waldhorn 16', Trumpet 8', Sw. to Gt. 8'
Gt. Diapason 8', Harmonic Flute 8', Octave 4', Twelfth 2⅔', Sw. to Gt. 8'
Ch. Festival Trumpet 8'
Ped. Bourdon 16', Violone 16', Octave 8', Gt. to Ped. 8', Sw. to Ped. 8'

Gt. Organ Registration + Strings
Ch. Trumpets, Trombones

54
ten.
poco a poco rit.
ten.
ten.
Gradually open Crescendo
58
ten.
Full Organ
Maestoso
Gt.
61
64
ten.
molto rit.
ten.

For the wedding of Kathryn Elizabeth Salley and Michael Dodd

Regal Trumpet Tune

Sw. Viola 8', Gedeckt 8', Principal 4', Piccolo 2', Mix. IV
Gt. Diapason 8', Bourdon 8', Octave 4', Spitzflote 4', Sw. to Gt. 8'
Ch. Festival Trumpet 8'
Ped. Bourdon 16', Violone 16', Octave 8', Choralbass 4', Bassoon 16', Gt. to Ped. 8'

Carolyn Hamlin (ASCAP)

Stately ♩ = 96

10
13
16
Add: Sw. Bassoon 16', Trompette 8', Clarion
Gt. Mix. IV
Ped. Diapason 16'
19
Gt.

23
26
29
33

Opening registration
37
Gt.
40
43
46

Sw. Viola 8', Gedeckt 8', Principal 4', Piccolo 2', Mix. IV, Bassoon 16', Trompette 8', Clarion
Gt. Diapason 8', Harmonic Flute 8', Octave 4', Fifteenth 2', Mix. IV, Double Trumpet 16', Trumpet 8', Sw. to Gt. 8'
Ch. Festival Trumpet 8'
Ped. Diap. 16', Bour. 16', Violone 16', Oct. 8', Fl. 8', Choralbass 4', Bombarde 16', Trompette 8', Gt. to Ped. 8', Sw. to Ped. 8'

62
65
With grandeur
Full, with Reeds
poco rit.
Gt.
69
73
poco rit.

For Lyndell Leatherman

The King of Love My Shepherd Is

Sw. Bourdon 8', Oboe 8', Trem.
Gt. Diapason 8', Harmonic Flute 8', Spitzflote 4'
Ch. Gedeckt 8', Viole 8', Viole Celeste 8'
Ped. Bourdon 16', Ch. to Ped. 8'

ST. COLUMBIA
Ancient Irish Melody
Arr. by Carolyn Hamlin (ASCAP)

In a serene, pastoral style ♩ = 84

13
3
17
21
slight rit.
Gt.
a tempo
25

* Sw. Flute 4', Trem.
Gt. Harmonic Flute 8', Gamba 8'
Ped. Lieblich Bourdon 16'

Where streams of living water flow...

*Sw. Trumpet 8'
Gt. Principal 8', Octave 4', Twelfth 2-2/3'. Fifteenth 2', Ch. to Gt. 8'
Ch. Gedeckt 8', Principal 4'
Ped. Diapason 16', Bourdon 16', Octave 8', Ch. to Ped. 8'

*Sw. Bourdon 8', Principal 4', Piccolo 2', Mix. IV, Trumpet 8'
Gt. Principal 8', Harmonic Flute 8', Octave 4', Twelfth 2⅔', Fifteenth 2', Mix. IV, Sw. to Gt. 8', Ch. to Gt. 8'
Ch. Gedeckt 8', Principal 4', Octave 2', Quintflute 1⅓', Scharf III
Ped. Diapason 16', Bourdon 16', Violone 16', Octave 8', Choral Bass 4', Mix. IV, Gt. to Ped. 8', Sw. to Ped. 8'

* Sw. +Waldhorn 16', Clarion 4'
Gt. +Double Trumpet 16', Tromba 8'
Ped. +Bombarde 16', Trompette 8'

Ped. +Bombarde 32'

For Dr. Jerry Aultman

Postlude on Austrian Hymn

(Glorious Things of Thee Are Spoken)

Sw. Bourdon 8', Viola 8', Principal 4', Mix. IV
Gt. Diap. 8', Harm. Fl. 8', Oct. 4, Twelfth 2⅔', Fifteenth, Mix. IV, Sw. to Gt. 8'
Ch. Festival Trumpet
Ped. Bourdon 16', Violone 16', Octave 8', Ged. 8'

AUSTRIAN HYMN
Franz Joseph Haydn
Arr. by Carolyn Hamlin (ASCAP)

10
13
16
19

Sw. Bourdon 8', Viola 8', Principal 4', Piccolo 2', Nazard 2-2/3'
Gt. Diapason 8', Harmonic Flute 8', Octave 4', Fifteenth 2', Sw. to Gt. 8', Ch. to Gt. 8'
Ch. Gedeckt 8', Viole 8, Principal 4', Flute 2', Sw. to Ch. 8'
Ped. Bourdon 16', Violone 16', Octave 8', Ch. to Ped. 8'

A little slower

Gt. +Mix. IV

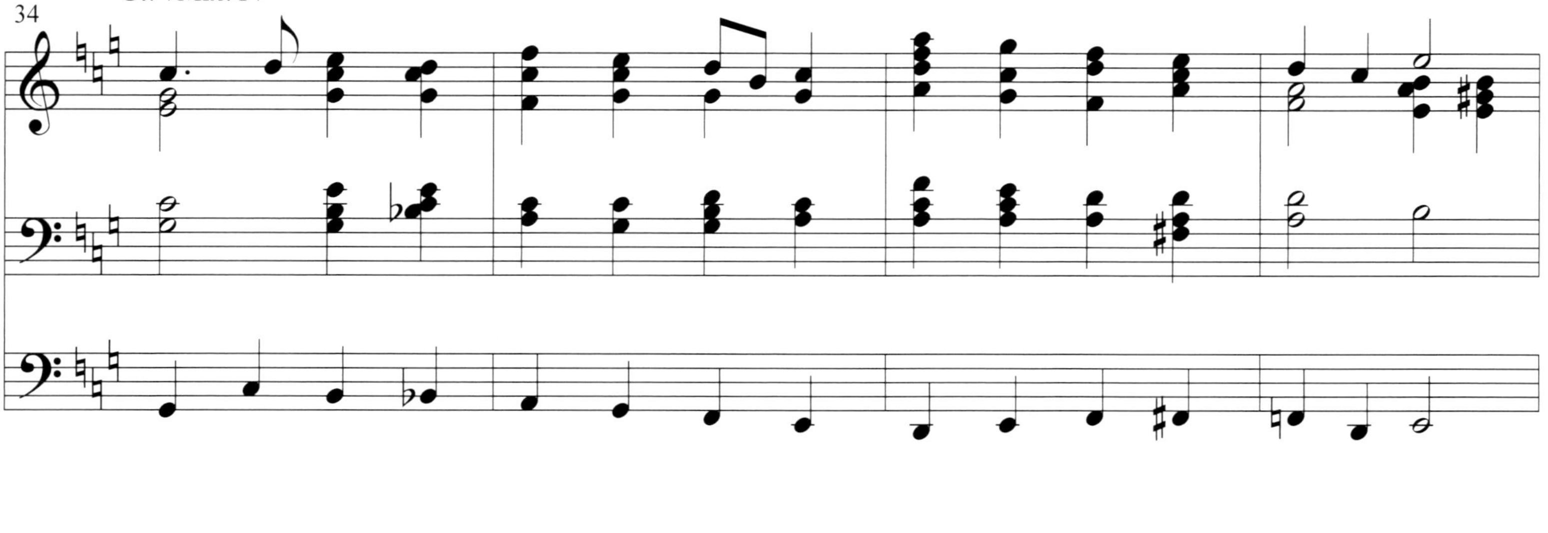

Allargando
38
Sw.
42
Ch.
46
Gt.
50
rit.

Sw. Bourdon 8, Viola 8', Principal 4', Piccolo 2, Mix. IV, Waldhorn 16', Trumpet 8', Clarion 4'
Gt. Violone 16', Diapason 8', Harmonic Flute 8', Octave 4', Twelfth 2⅔', Fifteenth 2', Mix. IV, Sw. to Gt. 8', Ch. to Gt. 8'
Ch. Gedeckt 8', Principal 4', Flute 4', Octave 2'
Ped. Diapason 16', Bourdon 16', Violone 16', Bombarde 16', Trompette 8', Gt. to Ped. 8', Sw. to Ped. 8', Ch. to Ped. 8'

Opening tempo (♩ = 120)

67
71
6
6
Full Organ with Reeds
74
broadening
deliberately
a tempo
78
slowing to the end

Worship Hymns for Organ and Brass

Music for Organ & Brass

A Mighty Fortress Is Our God	Arr. Bish/Nichols	BGK1088
All Hail the Power of Jesus' Name	Arr. Hamlin/Nichols	BGK1085
Christ the Lord is Risen Today	Arr. Hamlin/Nichols	BGK1042
Christmas Fanfares	Arr. Mark Shepperd	BGK1058
Easter Fanfares	Arr. Mark Shepperd	BGK1059
Festive Fanfares	Ed Wilmington	JH1280
Hymn Fanfares	Arr. Mark Shepperd	BGK1060
Hymn Fanfares Vol. 2	Arr. Mark Shepperd	BGK1061
Joyful, Joyful, We Adore Thee	Arr. Richard A. Nichols	BGK1053
Lift High the Cross	Arr. Hamlin/Nichols	BGK1041
Noel, Noel, Noel	Arr. Hamlin/Nichols	BGK1050
The Star-Spangled Banner	Arr. Hamlin/Nichols	BGK1045
We Gather Together	Arr. Hamlin/Nichols	BGK1051
We Praise You, O God	Arr. Hamlin/Nichols	BGK1087

Worship HYMNS FOR ORGAN